WINTER NIGHTS

COLLECTED POEMS

RONALD HADRIAN

Made with ♥ on the Notion Press Platform
www.notionpress.com

To those teachers and poets who introduced me to poetry

School:

Ms. Vidhya and Mr. Stephen

College:

Dr. P.Seethalaxmi and Dr. S.A. Palanisamy

You taught me the power of poetry.

&

Ko

Contents

Contents

Contents

Contents

Preface

To write poetry is to be vulnerable.

Some drink, some do drugs, but for me, the way to cope with pain and disappointment from an early age has been through poems. I have read and written them in the darkest times of my life.

"Winter Nights" is a poem I wrote for my dad. He was dying of cancer, and all I could do as an 11th-grade student was hope for a better tomorrow. I wrote that poem with faith, and then it all came crashing down. Two weeks passed, and he was no more. The poem I had written, I placed in the coffin as a memory. So this book is special to me in many ways.

These collected poems consist of works from 9th grade until now. Yes, I have lost many poems, but what I have been able to compile and what I deem to be publishing-worthy, I have added to this collection.

Some poems are religious, some are mere observations, and some are about love—but most of all, they are all about me. Heartbreaks, unrequited love, being tortured and used by people have all turned into words. To write poetry is to be vulnerable. You have to let your guard down and reveal your weaknesses.

Poetry is a statement of truth.

Read these poems slowly, enjoy them, imagine them, and taste the pain as I lament in words.

As the years rollby, my poems have become more religious; I have not included them here, but it seems that I have been drawn to mystical poetry.

Read them, explore them, and let the words become a part of your life.

Acknowledgements

I would like to thank my English teachers and Professors for encouraging and teaching me to write poetry.

To my friends Niveditha, Bala, Krish, Madan and Vignesh, for encouraging me at all times.

To Dr. Govarthini for all the help throughout the years.

To the talented Ms. Nancy for her illustrations and proofs.

To Kathir for putting up with all my literary discussions and translating my poems into Tamil.

To my mom, sister, nieces and brother-in-law for their support and encouragement.

To Dr. Banu, Mr. Subburaj and my HOD Dr. Deepa Caroline for all the support throughout the years.

To Karpagam Institutions, Faculty and Students, especially everyone at English Academy.

Dr. Mahalakshmi for giving me a chance with the courses, and trusting me.

To My Research Guide, Dr. Anita for all her support and encouragement, and HOD Dr. Aseda from Nirmala College of Women for all the support.

I finally thank God almighty for the pain and joy, otherwise all these poems wouldn't have been written.

Other Works

Hiron the Dark Blood

Rosaline I love you, but Don't Tell your Dad!

Eve's Tomb

Diary of an Eccentric Ootian

1. BLOOD THIRSTY WORLD

My heart is filled with elation

When I ride on a pony, it is an illusion

I feel the air fill my ears - it is a sensation

The music in air, which is played for redemption.

The mountains mimic what I say

I am esteemed by what I do today

For life is a mirror I see everyday

We are rewarded by I and thy deeds of yesterday.

Vanity is skin why become beautiful

For pride and glory people duel

Rainbow will turn bloody red colourful

Surely if this world stays so awful

To be good there is only one thing to spare

Prompt peace and brotherhood everywhere

Every mortal in this world must swear

That love and kindness must be the watchword.

2. PHILOSOPHY OF LIFE

It is cold in the soul

When passed through the church hole

Haunted one, century old

Where myths frequently told

That spirits roam about

The place were once lava was forged

It still exits underground

It is not clear why

Because ghosts do cry

And graves do open at night

Where vampires are afraid of light

And owls hoot with a sight

Which makes mice fright

Where wolves eyes are bright.

Where ravens fly about

Singing a dirge

Rest in peace

To sleeping souls

And bones broken from its joints.

It has a clock, which shows

Nine. Everyday morning

When I pass through the church

Where the old haunted mansion

Stands with a will

Singing a song which

Makes me sad

By the trees might and tall

Worries me about

The past, present and future of us all.

3. WINTER NIGHTS

I still have fear in my soul
About this person
Who is of my own blood
In anger did he scold
I was so heart broken
But now he lies in bed
My heart understands his love.
As the days pass
I feel lonely and lost
My winter nights should pass
My anguish must die.
I should see him again
With wealth and health
As before in past
My mighty dad should come alive.
I pray and wish
God with bliss
Shower his grace
That he may walk again
With his head held high.

4. PURE HEART

My heart leapt at your sight
Before chained by childhood my heart
But now it is free
To come into you without sorrow
But my heart gained no welcome
Unto thy soul that golden thought
I wondered and examined my thought
Mistaken was I about your melody cord
I write my whole ink unto you
Shall never give up until I gain a welcome by you
Cherishing in memory about
Those days forget not those lovely days
Speaking things which were not my concern
Nevertheless, realising it a dream to contain
Mischief was I innocent was thee
The world concluded by seeing our innocent friendship,
which I never lied.

5. A BALLAD OF SEASONS

Far and wide, my spirit wandered
Sky and earth lightened
Seeking the gate of heaven
My body lies at winter seven.
Chained in this unpleasant world
Sitting on my grave so old
Thoughts of my life flashed
Soul and spirit merged.

Part I - SUMMER

Born in the third star
In the cold hills of Hiron
A young lad grew with pride
Of knowing only happiness.
Alas, Satan nearly won
Sharp stone bored his head
Blood painted the wet earth seed
The lad nearly lost his life
Angels of heaven held his fall
Lord pitied him and granted life
For forty more years before winter seven.
Dumb, loon considered by all
Ugly, fat and considerably tall

The young lad reached teen
Ninth grade, Percy's at thirteen
Life changed when Ruth came
Love and romance next scene
Solitary, melancholy stood he
Three girls passed happily
The far end, pink robed she
The lad looked at her eyes with glee
Cute, beautiful and brilliant
Pretty, lovely and enchanting
The lass took the lads heart away
Like wind gently carrying light clay.
Her eyes, the most precious
Like the green emerald of Hiron queen
The rings in her eyes tell life
The inner spirit, outer soul
White, the mortal world
Her hair glitters brown
When sun shines its beautiful ray
Her lips formed with time
Like red flower buds so fine
But lovely than the three
Her smile makes Marcus see
His inner self and destiny.
A year passed like wind
Marcus was close to speak
On a sunny day end of week

'May you miss, lend your geography!
My teacher wants essay quickly'
The words echoed the whole week
Her smile embedded in his memory
Those words began their friendship
Before end their hands shook
Making a pact of friendship.
After two months of leave
The lad and lass returned
Attracted the poles commonly
On a certain hot afternoon
Marcus strode with Ruth
'Wait, I will bring my parch'
Spoke Ruth in sudden
Instead of Ruth, baboon returned
Delighted to see a boy like him
He ran from the place praising
First joke of Ruth that wonderful scene.
Mirth, laughter between them
Snares of teachers put venom
'Marcus stop the speech
With that little witch '
The words pierced his heart
Sadness beyond his wrath
Neither him nor her
Neither Marcus nor Ruth
Neither lad nor lass

Never looked at each other
Terrible nights the lad spent
Thinking about his friend.
Life took a turn,
Friendship took a turn,
Separation between them
Provoked love in his heart
Never revealed until summer ten.
Last day at Percy's term
Sat near his beloved one
'Sorry Miss, I be lying
Friendship won't be saying
Beautiful art thou
Queen Evans, my darling
Simple but powerful words
I love you my dear daring'
These words shocked her
Blushing and staring
Ran away without an answer.

PART II- AUTUMN

Sixth star she retuned
Marcus asked the answer
Ruth answered with a nod
Marcus delighted and happy
Ran in July wind ran wildly
Sat alone in James square
Ruth and Marcus vowed

Until death they love
Behind flew a dove.
'Dear Ruth I have to leave
Your beautiful eyes I will not see
Three years I have to be
Away from you but promise me
Wait till I come don't be deceived
I will return after I achieve
My wildest dreams of mischief'
Marcus kissed his Farwell kiss
Ruth's eyes made a wish
Only for Marcus she will live.
Three miserable years flew
Ruth waited and thought he would
But time elapsed, six years moved
Like seasons in perfect could
Lord Abin took her hand
In marriage she forgot and sang
'Marcus a boy loved me
He promised means nothing to us
I will love you even he comes to see
This heavenly matrimony'
Marcus was beside her
He tore his robes and swore.

PART III -WINTER

Resolved desolation and silence
Locked himself in tower talons

Never ate, never prayed

Heart robed in thorn named

Die Abin

Die Abin

On the other side of Hiron

Ruth cried and cried

Cursed her birth and wept

Her health lost and gone

Marcus, the only medicine she asked

Lord Abin sought and found

Marcus in his desolated home.

'Come, Ruth loves you

In her dying bed she lies

She might live if you

Come and embrace her alive'

That instance Marcus father

Eaten by invisible cursed worms

Lay in his wives arms

'Lucy this world will betray

Trust god and pray

There is always a way

Marcus take care your mother

If I die, embrace her

God is calling me near'

Oh, damn! That selfish lord

Took his father under his eyelid.

Leaving his crying mother

Hurried to Ruth Evans swiftly
Silently lay Ruth chanting his name
Marcus placed his hands upon hers
Moved closer and watched her eyes
Eye upon eye, hair upon hair
Nose upon nose, lips upon lips
Marcus kissed her his farewell kiss
Last breath of Ruth, Marcus inhaled.
Depressed, sad and mad
Opened his heart and searched
Philosophy and love of life
Inner spirit, outer soul
White the mortal world
First, seek the white
Man against man, country against country
Mortals learn from mine
Dark days yet to come
Love lost its meaning
Nature against it law put
Revenge upon us all is brightly lit
Second, seek the soul
Wisdom is supreme
God in wisdom
Remember wise folk
God is in heaven
And you on earth
Count the days of your life

For he is the ruler of life

Thus let your soul be humble.

Third, seek spirit

No man knows what spirit,

Which spirit, who spirit is,

Thus, Marcus concluded

Inner spirit, outer soul

White the mortal world

Ruth's beautiful brown eyes

Compressed them all.

On a windy day

Stood upon a rock on a valentines day

Above the roaring waves

Beneath the hollow caves

A gentle wind pushed Marcus

His last words

'Lord forgive me, Ruth remember me'

He drowned in winter seven.

PART IV - SPRING

Spirits also cry, you know why?

Thoughts of love and joy die

My death was an unexplained one

Deep under water, there was no sun

My body buried under this grave

I sit and cry about it in vain

Neither God nor Satan came to fetch

This lonely spirit of Marcus, the wretch.

It was spring
I heard heavens bell ring
Came angels in their enchanting wings
Grabbed my hand and showed paradise
Lord sat in his golden throne
His hand held a glass leaf sworn
'Marcus, your sins are forgotten
Sleep in paradise among cotton
Ruth and Marcus marriage in heaven'
They lived eternal in paradise
Ruth and Marcus with no worries
Summer, autumn, winter, spring
Finally Ruth Marcus love they bring
My winter nights I sing.

6. ODE ON MICHAEL ANGELO'S MOSES

I

Hundreds! Throng to see, his stern, bearded face
Some wonder at his majesty, others mumble disapprovingly
"It is unlike him," they mutter with a dreadful gaze
Others, struck with awe, drink his genius soothingly.
Toil, intense drudgery- for virtuoso is costly
David, Pieta and Sistine chapel, Oh bravo Angelo!
Thou hast not created Moses vainly
For Moses is a great attraction in the museum Angelo
But Women, Sculpture critics, sadly talk about Donatello.

II

He held him in his mind before eternity
Clay, erect stone, some chipping then –corner stone,
Working tirelessly, years and years before festivity
Alas, all creatures in Eden cursed then –hail stone
For he fell, yea, this original rock!
Never him but other half –doubting eternal Word.
Between life and fall, His Sovereign Smote!
Rib bone clothed in clay, feminine spirit with double-edged
sword.

III

Hail thy handiwork old man, your Prophet Moses is
Spectacular
The deliverer is seated with divine message oracular.
Yet, in humility he glows, this meek man with long beard

Oh! Euphoric joy to see him alive seized you Greybeard.

For, in spur-of-the-moment his knee you struck

And cried out, "Speak" and stood dumbstruck.

Critics lament thou mistake and caprice

Oh! Angelo, Angelo that strike made it a masterpiece.

IV

Perfection walked on this cursed world --this redeemer

The idea, fulfilment, the corner stone and head stone

Rejected by his own brothers and blasphemer

He hung on the tree, the maker of Moses

We esteemed him smitten; the world saw no beauty in him

But, Praise Him, for he saw him fit than seraphim

To strike at his side and take a bride who never loses…

For the enemies master temptations.

V

Greater than Moses, greater than David, greater than Solomon

The Great Sculpture's creation will not go rotten

It won't stand on a museum with a fractured knee

Critics lament and may even caprice it

But, Oh Lord, Lord that strike made it a masterpiece!

7. OCTOBER

October, a month of pleasant skies
Clouds like blue hills emerge on far highway road
The tedious, tardy life I follow
Is made easier and stored
The nebulous dance my brother does
The uncanny engine that I wish
Never started and throws
Smoke of misery on foes.

8. I STAND UNDERNEATH THIS TREE

I stand underneath this tree

Day by day wishing they would come and speak

The leaves have turned from green to yellow

I am still under the tree this willow

Like Buddha waiting for enlightenment

My days are passed—

Eureka Eureka! I cannot shout!

For I have found no joy at all.

This tree must have listened to my songs.

Smelt the canteen roasted snacks,

And heard the young children shout their alphabets wrong.

Alas, I am withering as you slack,

This intimacy with humans I lack.

9. SUDDEN ACCIDENT

Uncle, let us go for a walk—four o' clock
Let us talk about life, the experiences you had,
Or the way you felt before choosing your bride.
Whatever, just talk Uncle… I like to hear you…
What is it Uncle? Why are you so silent?
The wind is cold I know, forgive me,
I shouldn't have brought you out.
Wheels are screeching behind us Uncle!
Can you hear? You don't hear anything, do you?
You never heard my last words about my fiancé'
Yes, don't lie I know you never heard me—
You were busy being carried off the ground,
And smashing on the electric post—remarkable
Uncle! How did you manage to break it into three pieces?
Don't you dare give me that blank doubtful look,
I swear, it is the truth, I saw you as I lay there,
On the other side, wondering about this strangeness,
And why we both were bleeding,
And people surrounding us! Must be a bad dream Uncle,
Must be a bad dream, but before I could be sure,
I was falling Uncle
I was falling

Falling

Into utter darkness never to return again.

10. REGRETS

I couldn't stand beside your grave
Like I stood before 10 years naive.
Years have gone, and you are gone
I am imagining how it would have been.
Would you smile that I can pay my bills?
Would you be proud that I can use my skills?
I long to see your face when you read my books
To ridicule me about my poems or quips.
All the years you have been gone
Can we talk about it on the other side for an aeon
I, mom and sis, miss you a lot
I know I have promises to knot
But for now, Your memories are all that I have got.

11. A POEM CALLED THE CLOSEST THING TO MY REALITY

I imagine many scenarios-
The closest thing to my reality
Unbelievable, impossible, finally Adios
From everyone I adore with sincerity.
My imagination, my safe haven
Even when in reality; she is with another
In my mind, we still stroll across heaven
For none to judge, nor enemies to bother.
This blissful union in an illusionary world
Will be regarded as madness by some
The fortunate have their dreams unfurled
And in reality they walk with them.
Alas, the rest who imagine scenarios-
Pitifully, hold on to their memories
As that is their closest thing to their reality.

12. THE DECEMBER RAIN

The winter has come stumbling

Yet, the rain is lashing

The cold seems to be crippling,

And I think of my home with longing—

The memories are lingering,

I think of the cold, and dreading

I used to love with a mix of Melancholy and rage!

While I was meandering--

The verses would come forth,

Like drips from the ceiling

Then they would pour- like

Those from a bucket

Onto the already wet Cementing

I want to go back home

To hear the bang of the willow trees breathing

I want to smell the eucalyptus

As the piercing wind passes me storming!

Oh my, this plain wretched city has vaguely become my town

Just for a moment I know I am dreaming,

It is like shifted time-

I feel like I am once again in my Elysium sleeping.

13. SHAKESPEARE'S LOST SONNET

I've planned, wished and yearned

For Her to be a part of me

Lies, deception and fraudulent man, she screamed.

Severing our bumpy relation like a parted sea.

"Who is this Petra and Desdemona?" She cries.

"Why do you write about them so passionately? "

"They are from history my dear", I sigh.

"And they are virtuous women," I blurted.

Carelessly.

"Don't you think I'm virtuous,

You hypocritical bard of Stratford-on-Avon

I'm the one who makes meals so sumptuous.

I will proclaim your Iago heart to earth and heaven."

A special mention in my will-for this reason.

Just the bed for you-and the rest for your dog bottom

14. SONNET ON TAJ MAHAL

Pilgrims patiently placidly wait at the door
Imagining immaculate impeccable beauty.
Hearts flutter, fixated fascinated at Taj lore
The white marble, marvellous for its amenity.
From here, I hold like once my palm the proper substrate
I draw near, monument grows bigger, instils fear
No longer I hold, except cheap magic photos, I prostrate

I stand still, silence, 'I hear you laughing dear.'
Possessed, bereft of reason, I cross the guards
The cool marbles I trod, sweating and swearing
What happened to the wind? Where are my lords?
I reached our tombs, wake up once more my darling.
'Ticket please' my day dreaming diminishes at all events
I look into her eyes and wonder if she would accept my
monuments.

15. PASSER-BY

I stammer, convulse and fear her eyes

She is so near, yet she is far and cold as ice

I didn't intend to tell my dreams

She mistakenly mixed reality with fantasy themes

She reproached me of staying in a dream

A world she knew very little about

I stayed quiet- "My God am I only a book worm to all?"

I relaxed, and started to tell my true history

Just a fragment will do- I continued

She listened, perhaps giving life to my words, In her mind's eye!

She didn't notice but I was noticing her eyes..

Fixated in some far away oblivion.

What was she thinking? Did she know? Will she ever know?

What I was thinking... perhaps not!

I am hiding, hiding behind words,

Someday she will understand what I was saying.

Like a mist, she will fade...but I am determined.

Hold on to memories, and immortalize them.

"Don't call me brother," for her it is always a joke.

She teases, I act too, as though they didn't hurt.

but what use foolish me, I will vanish far into eternity and no one will find me there, nor she!

I might just be a passer-by for all!

What hurts me most-- I will also be a passer-by for her this

damned fool!

16. A POEM ABOUT MY HOMETOWN OOTY.

Can any other place be compared to my town?
Beautiful, green with serene blue mountains.
The mornings are a delight with clean blue sky zone
The way uphill to my town is full of sporadic fountains.
The birds that twitter in the morning
The owl that hoots at the dead of the night.
All are telling, and warning us of something
Destroy the town they will be gone out of sight.
Tourists throng and marvel at her beauty.
Gardens lakes, roses and eucalyptus trees.
The people are loving and caring and bask in her majesty
She is the Queen of hills they know of her overseas.
But, alas I fear the worst at present.
They are ravaging her, she is in her slow descent.

17. THE NIGHTINGALE

The nightingale I heard, so sweet,

Feels like I wasted time in hopeless dreams.

So melancholy, so dear my heart raises

From the shadow of death and lost ways.

Oh, nightingale, nightingale could you tell,

Give me hope by your melody cord

Ignite my spirit which is dead within me.

Take me away by your voice further than any dream.

I admire you and wonder by the window frame.

Who created you, tell me, my heart yearns to see him.

Tell me if I would cross yonder.

Will I see thy creator and mine I ponder.

You sway as though you are happy

Give me hope so I might also see

I forget my anguish and sorrow

Because I know thy creator also cares for me.

18. LOUDER THAN MY THOUGHTS

There is nothing louder than my thoughts
There is nothing that could handle this chaos
Inside my head.
Nothing, I repeat—nothing
There is a screeching scream
And there are these wanton dreams
Scribbling unclear words.

19. ODE TO SUNSHINE

O' mild Sunshine, welcome to my humble abode
This mind of mine is dark and sinister
With untold tales of loss and dirty wardrobe.
Shine forth your life giving rays and revive me,
Penetrate every nook and corner you desire
Console me with your presence and encamp me
Like Angels who look after the righteous.
This dreamy shine of yours camouflage
In ways that I could never imagine, Citius!
Your kindness to bring life to this deadness
Is like our Maker's faithful love
Ever tarrying for the repentance of the sinners.
Oh Majesty! You are a double - edged sword,
Mild enough to bring life, strong enough to burn cities
Yet you have humility, to shine forth by the Word of the Lord.
Day in and day out, you follow your course
Never straying to the right or left
You do your duty with a perfect force.

20. AFTERNOON SLEEP

Lying down with a book, pulling the pillow up
I lay down to read few lines.
My thoughts were agitated, the walls looked antiquated
I felt wearied in confines.
This temporary escape, takes an amorphous shape
dressed to the nines.
Then the walls turn to ghouls
Asking for signs.
Signs about the end, and how they ought to spend
Their time in decline.
I woke up, still the book beside my head,
and it said, read between the line.

21. THE FLOWER'S LONGING

I rejoice, I rejoice the rain has come

Oh, how gently she sent her breeze,

Wooing me, to raise my petals and sing.

Come love, kiss me with a drop

Softly now, you don't want me to fall.

Sway me with your wind and shout with your thunder,

That you love me!

Oh, poor helpless flower I am,

You can give me life and you can take my life as well.

Gentle dear rain, I am not strong as your other lovers,

Those wild shrubs and wealthy trees.

I am weak and my little body shall whither, if you don't come

again.

But I warn thee, don't delay longer, for you shall never find

me,

For I will be gone into the ground and will never rise again.

22. PRINCESS OF FLOWERS

Like a breath of fresh air she walks
The room begins to smell of her fragrance
She sighs that an intruder has come
Shooing away the eerie unwelcomed dove.
The dove keeps whispering his love
Sometimes the princess smiles at him,
Other times she says proudly about some new Raven,
Like she wanted to stir jealousy of this Dove.
The Dove understood all her intentions
The raven had taken his place in his absence,
The Princess of Flowers wanted the dove admonished,
So the dove left them in peace.
It's been ages
The Princess forgot, the dove remembered
Every colour of love the Princess created
In her grave the dove dropped every coloured flowers
And gave up his life there, in unbearable loss.

23. NET EXAM EXPERIENCE

The day begins with nervousness
Some speak in hushed voices, others
Showing off their tiny bookish Knowledge—
Only when a beautiful girl passes them by.
I stand alone- third time,
Thinking if I will ever clear this ordeal,
This stint.
First session-general, math and grammar
Will clear them in a breeze.
Second session- Alas, I would be
Like the cat on the wall or tress
Then lunch- not heavy fearing sleep.
But it comes, as I stagger through
Questions eleven to fifteen.
Not a single answer I know- yet
I am blindly swinging some.
Only God knows if I will clear
This exam this time.
Or, I will come again- and write another
lousy rhyme.

24. MY ABSOLUTE

Actual his word, absolute is He
Him I love,
For me his will- conclusive
In his love, I consummate
His word-Infallible-decisive sword
Thank him I must, unequivocally,
Hallelujah, Lord, my Absolute.

25. A GIFT

There was a poor old tramp living with his daughter,
His wife had died some years shorter,
He was weak and miserable and none hired him,
He made some cents and his face was grim.
What he made was never enough, even his daughter
Worked as a doffer.
The poor old dad cried desperately.
"Daddy, get me a doll this Christmas," she cried.
I have no money, he sighed.
"Daddy promise me a doll," she cried.
He promised but she died.
The dejected father, wandered hopelessly
Talking to his dead daughter damply.
Christmas arrived and he bought the gift,
A ragged doll for some few cents.
He didn't want to go home- and so he sped,
Listening to cheering crowds, and ringing bells overhead.
He kept walking away from them all.
He wrapped the doll carefully in his shawl.
The blistering snow covered his head,
Still he continued…not knowing the way or wither it led.
Next day, sobered up, they came,
These men of wealth without shame,

To the end of the alley,
There lay a man, a poor tramp, clutching a doll.
These men nodded their head, and said,
"Poor man, he never made it home,
Poor, ragged doll, must have been a gift to his girl's tomb."
The only way, the only way he could give,
His gift and keep his promise,
Was to die, and take it to his daughter in bliss (heaven).

26. TO MY NIECE

"Ma-ma" she calls and mumbles
"Ba-Ba" she sings and stumbles
"Paatuuu Podu", she wants to see YouTube
Builds her lego set and laughs as it crumbles.
I often wonder from whence she came
An Angel from heaven must look the same
"Ma-ma" she calls as I am in a call
"Bal-ha, Bal-ha" she screams as I throw the ball.
I understand her two-syllable words
Than all the epics of the world
Refreshing, innocent- God's own smile
Etched in memory even if apart a thousand mile.

27. LIGHTNING STRIKES

Love and death are like lightning strikes
Just a flash then the rumble
Two eyes meet- heart thunders with love
When eyes close- the laments rise slow
The love magic is in the flashy light
The understanding comes a little later
The sudden deathly fall is a sight
Despair comes a little later.

28. JUST MAYBE

Just maybe you and I
Lived together forever
On the mountaintop
Playing cloud games
And singing made-up songs.
I will love you with my whole heart
In summer and spring
Our kids will sleep with sheepling
Drink in cool streams of paradise
And play ice hockey with the Gods.
We can talk about anything
Or kiss for eons of time
Or sleep like hibernating bears
As the mortals pay their EMI's.
Just Maybe you and I
Can live in a dreamy world
before they come and bury us alive.

29. I IMAGINE

I imagine a life with you
But you will be living with your lover
Forgetting this fool who feels, thinks of you
Pushing me away like I am not worth a dollar
I used to live in the imagination
A nation which had flowers and poetry
Now is barren like Waste Land
Working mindlessly racing the clock of sand
To forget, to forget this childish pain
Goodbye, marry and be happy
Wonderful! farewell speech she will give
I will hold my tears, but with my voice clear
I will tell, God bless you dear
And disappear, never be to found in your life again
Until then I imagine that you and me are lovers!

30. HOW TO UNDRESS A GIRL

Rain Splashed, Thunder Crashed
Drenched she came home.
I peered at her
Made some coffee and sat down
No Towel, No Shower
She just wanted to lay still
I carried her to the bedroom
Put her on the bed and she said do as you will
I removed the top button of freedom
The other buttons of sexuality, individuality and wisdom.
I was excited to see her navel
So I stripped all her dreams
Lusting to see her bare bones.
Rain splashed, thunder crashed
Removed her pants of breath
Naked she lay,
Like a lifeless doll;
While I caressed.
Her dead body and soul.

31. MY LIFELINE

Darkness surrounded me
No way to escape, yet delivered me from oppression..
As light He came
I let go of my obsession.
Friends, foes all failed
Yet, He loved me without hesitation.
My flimsy heart made all the mistakes
Yet, saved me from all temptations.
I didn't merit any of it
Yet, He gave me salvation.
Someday He will come,
That day will be jubilation.

32. NEW SPROUTS

My mother and my neighbour (a pregnant girl) are friends
This rainy season they are off on an adventure
Everyday, they tie their hands with plastic bags
And rummage through a stranger's farm finding mushrooms,
spinaches, and wetlands
I watch from a distance as they search for the healthy greens
And chase away hungry sheeps.
They bend and stand upright and don't sing like Wordsworth's
solitary lass
Yet, in this south Indian autumn, the feelings of poets are
ridiculously same.

33. EXPECTATION

You expect they will miss you
You expect they will cry, you
Surrendered yourself , you
Changed yourself, you
Fell for the smile.
You now curse yourself, you
Hurt yourself, you
With your what if, you
Finally died.

34. CHOICES

Two roads will diverge in everyone's life
But one must choose his own strife
The good, the bad, the ugly are all part of the choice
A person must challenge with his own voice
The roads are filled with misty foes
Negating and crossing all the woes
Friends, lovers, heart breakers one must cross
Destination and destiny all depend on a choice.

35. FAR AWAY

Then
U and I close like magnets
Now
Far away, uncaring like strangers
Then and now everything has changed
Now and then, I wish to hold your arms and hug you until
eternities end.

36. OLD AGE CAN BE A CRUEL THING

Old age can be a cruel thing

It can cause heartaches in a blink

I've seen my mother carry us in a swing

But now, one hand on her hips and another on the sink

It pains my heart to see her grow old

With all those diabolical pains in her wrists and bones

Alas, old age can be a cruel thing.

37. I STAND AT THE EDGE OF THE CLIFF

I stand at the edge of the cliff

Waiting to make the deep plunge

Not a bone would survive the fall

Yet, I want to rest from this turmoil

The lingering memories and the pain

The never ending drama has fallen down the drain

If I disappear will she be happy?

Am I just a hindrance in her life?

Million heartbreaks and tears

For a person who cuts you with spears

Enough, a voice says.

Disappear and she will never find

Not your memories,

Or your life.

I stand at the edge of the cliff.

38. SUMMER IS DEAD WITHOUT MY PRINCESS

Summer, have you seen my lady?

She is a reflection of raw beauty

You think you are an epitome of anger

Let me introduce my Princess, the stronger.

The amalgamation of love and recklessness.

With her eyes she could torture,

And love, and make you want to hold her longer.

She is a heart breaker, and also a bone breaker.

She is more than you'll ever be, Summer.

She never nags like your mosquitoes

Nor drenches me with sweaty droplets

She simply ignores all the nonsense,

Like me, my verse and stupidity

Alas, the future can be a crisis

If I cannot compare thee to my princess.

I have no use for you, nor your dances.

Summer is dead without my princess.

39. DEPARTING

Both stood together laughing,
Bus arrived
She moved to the front door
Myself to the back, surprised
She didn't board , I did
I saw with unexplainable sadness
The bus pass her by
As she waved goodbye.
In life however,
I would be the lonely man on the road
She would be the girl on the bus
Waving me goodbye with some other man
She won't know a tormented heart
She won't know that she has left someone behind
She would be preoccupied with someone by her side
I would be a memory, similar to a person who recently died.

40. THOUGHTS AT 6.30 AM

She sat huddled with a cap on
So cute, that naturally I smiled
Here she was alone peering into her phone
While I stood near her trying my best to stay calm
For years I have known her
Yet, my heart raced like a hare
Wanted to talk but restrained
Didn't want her aggravated
She is so near yet not mine
She is intoxicating as pure wine.
I could write epics yet she will whine
That I have no rights, which sends sadness up my spine.

41. BLACK

Did you know that your eyelids are Black
A black hole to pull me in
No one will know where I'll be
After I pass through your black tunnel
Dispersed, shredded like paper
I would leap into eternity.
In grandeur you are clad
Like a panther.
I can see through the hips
Slender and calling,
Inviting to grasp you,
From behind.
As the lights diminish
We can be in each others arms.

42. THOUGHTS ABOUT MY MOM

When I think about all the people who truly love me
My mother would be the first.
She is the only soul, who would never leave.
Watching her grow old is a privilege
Her once beautiful face is wrinkling
Her long hair is starting to grey
Her knees are starting to hurt
Yet, in love she has grown stronger
I look at her and just say a silent prayer,
God let her never grow older.

43. DEAD DOG

What use is a dead dog
That lies in the street corner
Once it used to fetch a stick
Now it is stinking near the gutter
Once they petted it and even loved it
Now, unloved lies near the municipal toilet
All night it whined for help
but none came so it sucided.
The pain was unbearable,
so it crossed the street
exactly when a truck passed by it.
Kicking a dead dog to life
Is madness and a disrespect to the dead, Sire.
Oh, I am sorry you are kicking the dog
into the municipal basket
Then, by the way, Sire, tell the girl
who owned the dog,
to not forget this bulldog, as she plays with her new Poodle.

44. REMEMBRANCE

It is raining now and I am thinking of you,
Perhaps after many years,
When it rains I would be thinking of you.
I would be staring through the window
Imagining your pretty smile in the shadows.
I would be standing in a deserted room,
Cold and weak without hopes or dreams.
While I imagine your happy family all around you.
Remembrance of things past would hurt me too.

45. TO ALL THE PEOPLE WHO HURT ME

To all the people who hurt me
Made me suffer in the dark
For all the people who thought I won't become anything,
please spare a moment of thought.
For the girl who didn't love me
For having affairs with strangers
While I wrote love story from heart
For the people who body shame
Like they are immortal Gods
For the people who pretend to be friends
Just when they need any help of some sort
To all the guys who flirt with the girl I love
Don't you get it, it hurts a lot
Humans get hurt all the time..
In subtle and humongous ways.
Yet, the damage can be the same
The remedy is not wrist cutting,
Sleeping pill or falling off the edge
It is not death alone... That can cure my heart.
I need to torture you more with Love

While you hated, let me love
Your hearts will bleed someday when the world hurts you
And no one will be there to love.
So here am I, bloody and worn-out, death standing at the
gate. Yet I love!

46. THERE IS A CUP

There is a cup in front of me
Slimy, frothing liquid filled
The more you drink you will see
The white lights of heaven opened.
The poison gets to your head
Opens the reality that you're in
She is slipping away happily Wed
You slipping in nightmarish depression.
This cup of time, magically disappears
Drink and you will appear
On the other side lonely, lost, everlasting weeper.

47. I WAITED AND WAITED

I waited and waited
For the butterfly to come and be seated,
On me.
Just when she came to sit,
These frogs did croak
And startled this butterfly away.
I have to dance and prance and do
All sorts of gimmicks to lure her here
Alas these frogs have sent her away
Citing that I am not the one for her!

48. A DAY MEANS THOUSAND YEARS

A day means thousand years
When she is not here
I'm filled with thousand fears
As her absence kills me without a spear.
A day means thousand thoughts
Running like an ever stretching river
She is like a Kurinji flower in Western Ghats
Rare and wild yet a giver.
A day without her , thousand years
A day without her, alas, a thousands tears.

49. GREEN GIRL

On entrance she stood
Like a picture from a book
Clad in green , with angelic eyes
She smiled, and people saw her twice
Who is this parrot out of the wild
With dark red lips that would mesmerize even the blind
I tell all this but she never minds
But all this outside beauty would fade
But never her heart which is wild and kind!

50. THE RIDE

Hesitant she, nervous me:
As a princess, sat in my bike.
The road was long and tiring
But I was only dreaming
I could see her hair flaying wildly
Her eyes squinting at the scenery
She scolds me now and then
To keep my eyes on the road
How many days would I have imagined!
A dream came true,
But for her,
It was worrisome wondering if strangers eyes
Would judge her ....
These memories I store, deep within my soul
Like secrets that no one should know..

51. Y TELL ME?

Who else can I tell everything
When you are my everything
You ask why are you telling me
I want to share
Poems,
Gifts,
Sorrows
And suspense
All the subliminal things
Why should I tell you?
Telling you is my whole life narrative

52. CARNIVAL

Like a parrot walking in a carnival
She smiles and stares simultaneously
Like a child she spills the ice cream
And wipes the saree stained with pani puri
She enjoys local ice cream
And her beautiful pinkish lips turn blue stained.
Million eyes are upon her
Yet I cannot take mine.
Secretly following her eyes
Is tiring.
To others she is pleasant as angels can be
To me, a ferocious tigress ready to kill.

53. BE NOT AFRAID

O my soul, be not afraid.

You have seen you're beloved.

Her eyes are like doves.

She is the fairest among thousands,

Her silence liked by heavens.

Oh my most understanding queen.

Will you keep silence ever?

Will you never tell what you think?

About this poet who is sick in love with you.

You to me are the most beautiful.

My Juliet be quick in reply.

The lateness you show,

Is like I being close to death.

54. IN SEARCH OF LOVE

When little
I sought love
But none gave
(Even death took some away)
When a teen
I sought love
No crush even cared
When an adult
I seek love
But none truthfully cares
This seeking is tiring
I am looking for it in the wrong place
I had given it to people who didn't value it much
Then He came, this King, this Eternal one
Said he loves me when no one did
not vain, no expectation, just tailor-made.
In return, I love all these people with a Love
That they will never know.

55. EMOTIONAL ROLLERCOASTER

One day happy, one day sad
He will be okay they say
But these sad feelings are rusting his insides
Someday it will shatter him into pieces
and there will not come a happy day after..
Look, even a chain breaks at some point.

56. VACANCY

Before a week:
Phone calls to him was a burden
Petty fights was the norm
Irritating him was the sole entertainment
Now
Tears welled in her eyes when he called
Almost merciless sadness hung in her heart
She felt irritated by everyone around
Then love was playful
Now love is like a piercing sword
Then she never thought she will miss him
Now the separation makes her numb.

57. TWO IS ONE

Sick in love he stood outside the door
He knocked, and knocked
"Who is this?" she asked.
"It is me" he replied
"I don't know you, I won't allow you inside"
He bruised inside, went around the world
Took part in battle, hurt and humble he came
and he knocked and knocked after some years
"Who is this?"
"It is you"
"Now you understood. We both are the same"
They closed the door together.

58. TO FIRE AND ICE

She is fire
She is ice
Words like fire
To burn your heart alive
And words like ice
To melt your heart and entwine
She will push you aside with vigour, most of the time
And sometimes hug you tight, like her soul would merge as
one
I love both her eyes,
One is fire, one is ice
But I don't care
If I have both I have her soul in my hands.

59. KINDRED SPIRIT

Where were you all this time?
How did we not met earlier?
I only thought I was the weird one
But no, you were weirder than me!
We have many things in common
Like depression and sporadic tension
Sometimes lazy to the core
Other times, talk till our throat is sore.
Your laugh echoes through the room
It is magical as it's a rare carnival
You're nostalgic with books of doom
And energetic with books -motivational.
Introvert maybe to others
But not with kindred spirits
I'll miss you like an ocean without water
And song without sound.
So once again,
Farwell my kindred spirit.

60. FAITH

My old friend where have you been?
I miss you terribly
I was once fallen
Into this sinister depression
But you came and rescued me
Now again I am in need of thee
Need thy power to change everything
Yes my friend, come along with me
We can change the world...
If I have you, I know I can move a mountain.

61. RUMINATIONS OF ROMEO

I want to hug you so tightly till our souls would merge as one.

62. CHAOS OF CHOICES

Every word pierces like a dagger
While I try to stay calm
She is trying to subtly hurt me
Yet, there is care at every fixed eye
She is scared of consequences
Of allowing my hands to get too near
Holding her hands won't hurt her, but she will remember
The memories of past that is gone
I try to ignore these feelings
Fearing the obvious chaos of choices
I try to walk in a rope naively hoping the wind won't cross
It started as a whisper, now it is a battle cry for remorse

63. A GIRL CALLED SUNSHINE

This dark room suddenly erupts with light
Not a blistering one, but a maroon red
Drawn on the face of the sky
Delightfully beautiful to the beholder
She climbs steadily upon the heavenly stairs
And I gasp, awestruck by her presence
She spreads her enchanting rays over azure sky
And smiles like a merry young girl
Enticing me with her blinding light.
I dreamt and made plans
Like it was going to be the truth
But not realizing a dream must only end as a dream
I fought to turn it into a reality soon
Only to be stung by my expectations.
Why I carry this sunshine's memory
In this dark alley way!
Imagine again and again it will shine through
And find a place in my dark heart someday.
But in the end it is clearer than ever
For someone else all works for good,
And not for me, I understood.
On a pendulum my heart sways

Reaching far and wide

Never returning to the same position

Like before you entered my heart.

The weight of you pulls me deeper

Into oblivious darkness and thought

I clamour and swim

With a temporary sort.

Heat to cold and cold to heat

Nothing is certain

In this calamitous relationship,

I hate.

My god, how awful this imaginary

Relationship.

I must break away from such trivial

Sentiments.

Who has dared to touch this Shine?

A million fragments I would become.

Who has dared to kiss her wings

Flames will ever burn like torture.

Can a man tightly hug the flames?

And not get burnt.

It is of no use

To vainly, deeply desire her

She is sun and I am dust

Literary blossoms come out of this infernal earth

(Once the sun touches me with her presence)

I create words and words and bear fruits of tears

Nothing else

For the sun can parch the land

And leave cracks in heart and dust.

O' sunshine, thou majesty

The never conquerable, and never attainable

Behold, you cannot penetrate the deep earth

Where I will be buried, until my Saviour's return.

64. REMEMBRANCE

Nine years without you
Yet, the pain lingers
The best part of my life,
All missed by you--
Sometimes, I silently scream
questioning God about your end!
"He was a good man, wasn't he?
Then why such a suffering end!"
Nothing echoes back to soothe me.
I am lost in doubt and venerability.
"Responsibility is heavy on me,"
I whisper in my prayers
"Don't worry--look at the sparrows..."
You quote scripture, turning my heart to eternity.
Every time I think about you dad,
I am driven to stand like a man,
and fight this dog life, like a dog
that's mad.
Many years might come and go,
I can never forget the lessons
You taught me to grow and glow--
Simplicity, humility and kindness.
And the greatest lesson,

If I ever wanted to be great,
Yes dad, there is no getting around this,
I must be a servant to all my fellowmen
without selfishness.

65. HOW AWFUL THIS LIFE

You get punished for doing the right thing,
and the wrong.
I can't even sing a song,
my soul needs to fly, from
mediocrity up the sky
Uh, I sigh, and all the lies
torment me now.
Why life treats me this way,
I don't know.
This weird little lady, shouts and hysterically screams.
Entire class giggles and laughs about me.
I have become a clown and that much I know.

66. FACEBOOK

Facebook, thou ask me what is on my mind.

Let me give thee a piece of it.

It is ruminating on thy terrible question.

My mind is filled with lyrics of songs, characters out of books,

poetry and much trivial things.

But I can't post them, for the simple reason

of not being liked.

Thus, I post about scandals, photos of joy, but never of

sadness-

Afraid of social classification of being uninteresting.

But hear me now, I have to tell it all,

Thou waste my time with thy question,

My good time can be spent on books and not social media.

For thou ask questions and keep quiet,

But I want answers and I can get them in my solitary walks,

So, hereafter don't ask me questions- for I am not a bard.

67. HOLLOW MAN

He was a hollow man, a hollow man
A book lay open beside him, yes, the hollow man
He closed his eyes and listened to his heart,
Hoping he would hear life, within his hollow self
Lust, greed, self-righteous his virtue, this hollow man
Guilty, guilty grumbled his hollow heart
Friends, family, why even angels couldn't help
His hollowness.
He hide himself in his hollowness, his screams would echo
now and then.
Why, why? I tell you this because he is a hollow man,
And hollow man's deeds are echoed eternally.
Try to save him- fool! Fool! Hollow man saving another
hollow man,
Oh what a joke!

68. ONE MORE TIME!- A SONNET

Little boy lead him- the gatherings cheered
The purblind, once a lion hearted man stood.
They jeered-Philistines elated appeared.
Ashamed he groped- tears falling good
Killed he thousands with jawbone, they said,
Riddles, Delilah, amnesia spiritual,
Where was it? Without power he would be dead!
Heart to her he gave- mortal desire perishable.
He thought about his Nazarene vow, alas
Woe unto me he blubbered. They mocked,
Praising Damon their God en masse
He thought about God's power and stopped.
Just one more time Lord, let me avenge- he prayed
The heavens shook, down came the columns and slayed!

69. APATHY

I don't care for war
Nor for water scarcity someplace far
I sit in my humble abode
Listen to news and ads about some kabab
A self help guru talks about empathy
I've even heard politicians talk of sympathy
Clarify me if I'm wrong - but
I won't and don't care, pardon me
Even if no one loved me, or you forget to keep flowers at my
grave
I won't ask- now don't worry
Now, don't look at me that way
You ask, why I have become this way
I used to care, I used to care and care
Every atom of mine cared
For her, but she didn't
She I buried her along with my sympathy and empathy
And became the mirror image of apathy
For just a girl you say- pardon me sir
Remember, you are talking to apathy me

70. IN THE COOL MIST OF JUNE

The early morning commenced with rain
Dogs sleep huddled along the lane
I pity them they exist in vain
But what of me I have nothing but pain
At least the dogs huddle and sleep together
They trust each other whatsoever
But what of me no friends for or brother
I roam this selfish world in this silly weather.
What becomes of my dream every night!
Do they fly away as a broken kite?
Or is my heart just to light?
Or is my will too late to react?
Whatever be the cause I feel so last
I feel invisible and hopeless as a ghost
Betrayal and hatred with no remorse
How and life I got only before the cross.
I waited as the season slowly passed
Waiting from dust to dawn with dreadful loss
I'm the chill mist of June
My suffering would end every soon.

71. NAMESAKE

For name sake they talk,
They make fun and mock
They ask for the rope
When in deep oceans of doubt
But once they are out
They become your name sakes folk 'I will give my life for you
my friend'
Then, when it deep despair
The name sake friends are not there
Yet. Of them all, when you choosing to be
Name sake too
I want my very name to disappear soon.

72. DID TIME STOP FOR THEM

Did time stop for them
For these dead people
Are they happily enjoying?
The freedom from time's clutches?
Or waiting for it to end
Just like us.
But beware time serves Him only
In this time serve him well
Then beyond time, you will enjoy eternity, says one.
Enjoy for time waits for none
In this time be epicurean
Then beyond time, what would matter, says another
Did time stop for them
Perhaps it did
But my memories, never will
Of people who have slipped out of Time's kiss.

73. ONLINE

This online business is kinda bad
It can ruin peace in an introvert's mind
Checking constantly if they are there
Imagining all sorts of deceptive smear
Jealousy can aid this fear
Last seen is complete terror
Of you missing something, while someone is feasting
The great remedy is to jump out
Or hand in clutches to this virtual loop.
These people put masks of majestic beasts
But they can allure you to hells deep
These updates, smileys smile all creep
While these souls of dreams weep

74. A HOT SUMMER NIGHT

A hot summer night

I am longing to see your eyes

It's been a while

Peering into those Angelic brown eyes

Our conversations are about webinars

And Research papers and mythic Norse

But I don't want to talk about those

Truly I need to converse

Of stars, Mars and love songs.

But you would block

And push me away like I am a lost cause

But remember you can't

pluck me out, nor silence my eternal voice

It will echo about you, and you.. And you.

until it will haunt in your silence too

about a true love that you lost...

75. LOVE IS UNIVERSAL

A Black cat lived in our house
It purred, drank milk and snoozed.
One day it became a mother
With four kittens of different colour.
They all grew up quickly
And so the room became stinky.
One day my friend visited,
He took the favourite kitten unsolicited.
That night I couldn't sleep
My cat, searched, screeched and weeped
I could see love in the green eyes
Poor thing was helpless without a voice
My heart broke to see that sight
Of a mother's love at the middle of the night.

76. COUNT DOWN

For some count downs are celebrations
for others count downs are like waves crashing on rocks
breaking every bone of a fragile soul
It might be days, months or years
the power of abstract numbers inevitable!
Countdown for departings are most painful
Like leaving own shadow in a deserted cage.
But once the count down is over...
you can either choose to fall and drown or jump with faith
and show your beloved what they missed!

77. PAIN

My mother's neck has sprained

In pain she cries

Silently at midnight, so I wouldn't wake

My heart beats faster

I wake, and do whatever first aid I can

I pray for the sun to come

Watching her lie in bed with wreathing pain

Hesitantly call my friend

Curse myself for not getting a car

The doctor gives the medicine

We come back home,

I watch some reels to hide my worry

Then after 20 minutes with her weak body

She places the breakfast on the table

These mothers are crazy

Anger rose within me and then a disappointment, that I am

lazy.

78. THE GREATEST TRAGEDY

The only person with whom I share my good news and bad
news is you
but I don't know how long I have time
Like a person waiting for death, I wait
who will I share when I make a great deal?
Who will I share when I have a failure ?
(When you fail in love, nothing will make sense)
Who will listen to my insecurities?
I thought if you age, feelings will die
But they still sting...
I used to be a lonely man, then you came
A little light in the tunnel, but now you will go
then once again lonely, and in dark I will be
The greatest tragedy is not when you lose a loved one.
But to lose someone who never loved you.
I don't know what it means to be loved.
I just read about them,
it is a made up story.
Throughout my sad, and painful life
I have walked with God,
I guess once again after you're gone,
I can only walk with Him.

Otherwise my world will collapse

like a house of Cards.

79. DAYS WAITED AND WASTED

I have wasted all the days

Waiting for love.
I admired the beauty of the sky,
But couldn't hold it with my bear hands.
Felt the wind,
But could not kiss it.
Touched the ground, but cannot
Bore a hole.
She was all the elements;
I was only a man
I waited and wasted time.
Now I have grown weary
My ashes will be carried away
to the sky, by the wind and buried in the ground.
Then I will finally be a part of her!

80. LICENSE TO KISS

I warned you, you say
But how was our relationship
wild, uncertain, not friends not love
Somewhere in between
You let me kiss, feel breasts, thighs,
Eyes,
But don't insert your penis
My virginity is sacred.
But you can have me in your mind.
A joke isn't it... all this about feelings.
What does marriage mean? Life mean?
A joke. All a joke...
No purity, just a license to kiss.

81. MOLE ON HER NECK

How will the wind feel when it is restricted to touch the
blooming flowers
It would sigh and howl and hold its breath
All the possibilities will be shrunk to its imagination.
The wind would imagine stealing a look at a particular rose
It would create a tornado around it, yet it would not touch
the rose.
It would go insane and blow recklessly on the icy plains of
Artic.
Blow with anger and rise the waves into a tsunami
The love lorn fingers too wrestle with tsunami of feelings
He wants to touch the mole on her neck
And glide his fingers around it
Like caressing an ancient manuscript.
He wants to use it like a switch on her emotions
She would respond with a deep breath and fade slowly out of
consciousness.
While the wind blows the curtain part in jealousy
He parts her hair to kiss the mole on her neck.

82. VISIT FROM THE MUSE

I sit quietly trying to focus on my work
Her memories knock gently
Louder they become, stopping my thoughts.
She enters in, and lies on my shoulder first
Then looks at my eyes like she had never seen
a man.
Holding my hands until darkness spreads
from my pen
The Angel has left me with a bitter sour.
She made love in the meadows
and birthed some heart-breaking songs
Then she left the place without a choice
I wailed and waited.
Disguised as friend - she approached me many
times.
The memories like crumbling palace of the
Dream Lord
Held me in prison cell.
Powerless, I watched as she rode away with
brand new jewels
with a new Prince from afar.
Hoping Time would heal and drown all these

wounds

I travel on My Lord's narrow way

Lost Love is a small price to pay.

83. ON WATCHING A DRIZZLE

It drizzles gently

The dogs huddle near the warm diesel generators

The aroma of coffee gently climbs out

of the cafeteria

Students occupy the seats hoping to watch their dazzling

lovers.

It drizzles gently

I sigh within myself, the calmness

Carries my memories to the vacant hill station house

The image of rain outside the window

The hot buns with chicken stuffed in

make me hungry again.

The beans bowing down as water beats its head

The plums on the trees washed, the roses

aroma lost

It drizzles gently

I had no need to think of love or alluring lips of women

Innocence looked at the rain, and wondered if they would

declare holiday

But age looks at rain, and hopes for some companion to

cuddle in.

It still drizzles gently.

84. IT WAS YOU!

After all these years it is you.
The spark in my heart
the yearning, the sweat
in my brow... all for you.
My imaginary relationship,
My passion for you,
the million dreams about you
Uncensored thoughts for you.
I don't even notice others
for who will look at street lamps
When I can behold the Sun.
Can't love a street lamp
Cannot imagine!
My sun might descend, and I will be in darkness
Yet, I would dream about the Sun!

85. BROWN EYES

I think she borrowed eyes from angels
That dark brown, irresistible eyes
like chocolate melting
I want to behold and hold
As the waves crash against the shore.
Like boats rocking, then water leaking
Wet like chocolate from the coco plant
Fresh and aroma enticing.
Universe explodes when she fixates
those elegant eyes with mine.

86. CARE

I wish to care for you
like a dragon, its young.
Hold your hands
And assure you I am there for you
When you're feeling cold
Wrap you in my wings
while you rest comfortably
Comfort I will give,
Even though you despise my touch
With kind words,
As I don't have much.

87. GREEN

She was clad in green
she came like a dream
Like sunshine on a wintery day
like the scenery I admired
Her beauty inspired
a fire wrapped in a robe was she
She is wild yet caring
But sadly I wouldn't be spending
My life in the lush green tree
with her dressed in green.
But with jealousy thoughts I would sit
on a green mossy graveyard with a wish.

88. LOVE WAS ONCE

You shout that there is no love
Then why torment me all these year
If love had faded
You could have gone away
Sometimes I think you have used me
Even though there was no love
You stayed, and gave me hope
Alas, You waited till some dark lord entered
Now you are with someone else
But who can love,
Care, rejoice than me
You are just like the mere mortals
Then I realised
Love himself Love's me
I shall Lament, yet someday
As a prophecy
A great name I will have
Among all the mortal men.
And you my darling will be remembered
Only by my lines.

89. MINI EPIC

PART I

On the rainy days of June
Sped the young lad across the moors

Along with his sheep and cows
Fearing the attack of wolves
While he is gone away from home
He woke up after a dream:
The dream about fire and ice
And a beautiful girl he had never seen
The sky grew dark and petrified
When gigantic clouds covered the sky
He ran and kicked his sheep
And wondered what happened to the floating ship
That crosses the sky like a raft
On the troubled waters of Thames.
"It is just a dream, a dream"
He sped along the sloppy moors
To the wooden cabin up the hill
His humble aboard, his sanctuary
A small brook ran beside his cabin
Where he tasted water day and night.
Now, he locked the door
And hid himself under the cot
Tears trickling from his eyes
His heart beating in a rhythm
Of melancholy and terrified dance
Suddenly, the doors thundered,
The wolves, gathered....
Snipping, and growling their hungry growls
"please let us in," they spoke

Like the sly beast of Eden
They growled, yet they cajoled
"You will make us a good feast
Across the sky, you can quickly meet your bride"
They taunted, these sinister wolves
They waited and waited until
Another scent arose in the distance
These beasts raced across the moor
To behold a fair princess, white as snow.
She looked innocent, and the wolves were tamed
Then they carried her back to the cabin
"we got a present for you," they growled
Meanwhile, the lad had climbed a tree
And saw the fair princess tame the pack.
His heart beat like the thundering cloud
Love blossomed on the barren land
Waters of affection flooded the land
He jumped down, no more afraid of the pack
The fair princess laid her eyes on him
And the ground beneath him bloomed
With marigolds, roses, daffodils and lilies
The wolves carried the princess to the lad
"young man will you provide shelter," she smiled
The lad took her in; and blushed.
A tiny bed, some withered vegetables
A shelf of discarded magical books
Nothing more than the smell of the mud.

She sat in bed and asked for food
The lad rushed out, but a roasted hen
Already greeted him on the ground
"what kind of magic is this?"
He carefully carried the plate inside
For three days and nights he served her,
Admired her while she slept
Peered into her eyes while she awoke.
She asked him to take her to the fountain
Just a mile away from his cabin
The wolves were forbidden
Only he was allowed to see her bath
He wanted to touch her,
But his virtue chained his deceitful heart
When she came, shed echoed "you passed"
To behold the fair princess, yet restrain yourself
Is a Goliath task
So come I will give myself to you
In the cabin up the hills
He wrapped the princess in his arms
Feeling every inch of her soul and body
The beautiful hair held in his arms
He adored the princess
In ecstasy they held each other
Her lips came forth with milk
"I am dripping for you", she held.
While he poured honey inside her lips

Lost from the world- into the depths

They were one and the same

Fire and ice merged into his soul

When he lay beside her, he dreamt

About heaven – the white marigolds

When he woke up the cabin was dark

The Fair Princess was gone away

The wolves have vanished,

He cried again and again, he did

The emptiness killed him, and he stood

On the top of the mountain

And declared his name "Francis the stone"

The mountains trembled, and he screamed

"La belle dame sons merci."

He crushed the winds and sea

And summoned the flying ships.

The dragons awoke – the serpents slithered

The rivers turned bloody, the earth cracked

The ravens came with the news

"The Fair Princess now sits on her throne"

PART II

'Richard the stone' had grown into a man

Every morning he carried his cattle

Up and down the hills- strengthening his body

Thinking of the fair maiden fired his belly arms

Without a word disappearing- hurt his mortal soul

The floating ship was ready,

The wizard Merlin cast his spell
He warned that this voyage would start a war
Of mortals and gods
He took his trusted companions
Those who fought in the great Trojan War
Ulysses, Achilles and Agamemnon
All in ghost form, unable to wield a sword
They advised, and cajoled about the dangers toward
The floating ship named "Torobell" set sail
Crossing villages and hills, his heart made a leap
He would never return and he was certain of it
Odin the mighty Eagle served him well
Telling him about the whereabouts of Fair princess
"She is in the depths of the great forest", Odin whispered
His eyes flickered and he grasped the mast
He called the wind to lead him to greats
The ship floated for three days and nights,
At night he slept by the fire for -
Ever groaning with nightmares
About death and his winged dragons
Conquer me not, he cried
As the wings covered, he signed
With sweat he woke up
It was getting hot as the sun
The wind had seized – the ship (seized)
To move while it entered the great forest trees
"Come my Torobell, rage, rage, rage"

He hit the mast with all his strength

But Torobell, yielded not a cinch

The forest trees, tall as Herculean

Swayed but there was no wind nor breeze

For they were alive and fierce

Like an annoying bee over their head

The floating ship drifted ever so slowly

The trees loosing patience smote the rudders

Torobell shook and for a minute

Lost magic of the great Merlin

"What Impudence?" spoke Achilles

"If I were flesh and bones"

"I would burn these ugly woods to the ground"

"Peace," spoke Ulysses the crafty

"These woods have ears," he whispered

"Let me talk to them," and stood from eternity

I beseech thee – help us in this hour

For we seek to find the princess

The one who is prophesied to burn the world

There was silence for a day

Then the trees betrayed the princess.

They led them to the womb of the forest

She slept peacefully, innocent as a lamb

"Richard" anger burned, but vanished

In her presence his power vanquished

She opened her eyes, the sun rose

Birds chirped and sang – Richard froze

"What brings you here shepherd?"
She sighed and called her leopard
"My body, or soul or power"
For a second he imagined, the body
The milky white skin, the scar on the head
The dripping wetness of her body
The smell of her hair
The ever present fire in her eyes
She seemed to have read his mind
"Like all the mortal dogs?" She laughed
Richard felt a pang, a pounding heart
"Don't read my mind you witch"
"A witch, me a witch, you fool
I am supreme Emperess- "
"Order, order," shouted Agamemnon
"Supreme lies is all you say"
The fair princess smiled her pearly teeth twinkling
"When I was in your arms I saw a vision
The future of me and you
Night and day, I wanted to be with you,
Make love to my love, but Alas
A curse has been on me too
You are a shepherd, and I am a leopard
I am sure to kill you one day soon
The princess sang this song , unspeakable
Filled the atmosphere strong
"What have you seen," Richard begged

The days of war is ahead
The armies are marching instead
Death has come for us all-
Just a matter of time, this forest wall
Would lie ablaze
I will need all my leopards blood
To retain my life
And she killed the leopard of her lap
And licked the blood, in her knife
While the gods, in terror called Torobell
The princess vanished- the distant
Fire and song were her farewell
Part III
Torobell stood still up in the sky
While the fires raged and raged
The Ghost Gods gave out their sighs
And Pitifully looked on Richard the Aged
"Time" they thought -"that monster time"
Robs men their youth, and women their prime
Torobell had stood still for a week
Richard Felt aged and meek
The Princess was gone, but memories
lingered on his frontal lobe
The Gods to ease the pain, in reveries
showed Richard their youthful brawls
And beautiful women, in naked baths
Nothing eased the pain.

He wanted the Princess -like an infant
He demanded to the Gods
"Yes we are Gods but love and will
Are an individual's choice
Even Zeus in all his might
Cannot dictate love and the way of kite
The memories of the Princess hunted him
Day and Night he weeped
And water level of the oceans rose higher
The Gods cursed their birth
They vowed to avenge the princess - and her path
They sought an alliance with the wind and waves
"My friend the wind will lift me high" said the waves
"And crash me into the land
I will ride along with rage
Until I find the fair maiden
Until I carry her in my arms
And shake her cold heart out of her
I will put the fire out of her, I swear"
It seemed his sorrow, turned creation grim
Then Richard raised his hands
And Silenced the Gods and waves,
"She might not love me, but I do
Her heart might hear my weeping
And sprout with love someday
Until then I will hibernate" - like the bear
While he slept, the ship flew over the horizon

The Ghost Gods peered into the distance

One of the seven gates of hell opened

They marvelled at this sight

The gigantic door opened in the middle of the ocean

"Should we wake him up" Achilles asked

"No, but who would do such a diabolical thing"

Agamemnon banged his head on the mast

"She made an allegiance with Hel

And opened the gates of hell

The invisible creature would torment

The living souls would all lament

The Princess was right after all"

The night grew weary and Richard woke

Seeing the enormous hole of the ocean

And the Ghost Gods sore.

"What is this?" he mumbled

"The gate way to hell, and your beloved opened it"

A lightening of pain passed him

"Can we stop them," Richard Asked

"Only if we go in and dine with Hel"

Richard in a brave manner

commanded Torobell to enter the gate

Under the ocean they went

Each holding onto the mast for life.

Darkness covered them and then a light,

A grey, flimsy light emerged

Torbell levitated near the ground

The hell hounds barked and barked
Hel walked out, and saw the ship
"Who dare enters here? Declare yourself"
I am Agamemnon, accompanied by Achilles
"Dead warriors, come to rest on my lap,"
"No, daughter of Darkness, we have come with a mortal"
"This is no place for a mortal," she screamed.
"You are breaking every law of Gods, you dead Gods,"
"This shepherd is searching for the Princess of Flowers"
And they threw Richard onto the ground.
He bowed and watched the hounds encircle him
"I smell pain and torture,"
she touched him and saw everything in a flash
"She gave herself, and took it back
Along with your heart and soul"
Richard looked worn-out and sad
"She didn't care my elegant man,
She used you, and fled."
"That's a lie," Richard moaned.
"She is a mixture of fire and Ice
She can't help it.
She loved you, but also hated you
She is a paradox, a bundle of contradictions"
This curse of hers is wrecking chaos
"She opened the gates of hell,
and commanded my invisible demons to haunt the world
But she cries for her mistake, in a cave

Like a remorse stricken child, with the leopards in her lap

Be gone now, search no more

Return to your humble valley

And love someone who is worthy

Of your love and soul.

PART 4

Richard left the gates of hell

With dying pain and endless drain

In mind, in heart and at soul

Which cave has she hidden

This princess that once he knew

Was she tormented like him?

Or was she indulged in love with someone?

He cursed that day he met her

It was like a curse that followed him

Like a heavy elephant sorrow tormented him

Torobell flew across the sky

Raced with Odin's Eagle eye

But the earthlings below

Swelled and died

These invisible demons entered them

And ate their insides

Day by Day the plague spread

From one person to another

The gods and Richard viewed the horror

"Can't we do anything?" Richard cried.

The demons will only oblige to her

"Then we have to go find her," Richard cried
"Stop this madness at once."
"The madness in you is more deadly
How many more days you will hold on,
forget her, and let go," the ghost Gods pleaded
Torobell was entering the land of Mist
Nothing was visible, dark clouds,
A hum of danger, the Gods shivered.
"The Land of Mist, the unfortunates end up here,
The mountain of doom is ahead of us,
The only place to end immortal life is here,"
shivered, and squealed the Gods.
The Mountain of doom smoked and trembled
"Why would gods leave their immortal life,"
Richard asked in awe
How long to suffer the pangs of conscience
They give up their ghosts here
All the wrongs must end here
This is their doom, their penance
But once their fall, they never come back
Their memories become vague, and people forget
that these heroes ever existed".
Richard thought about it
"I have no hope and I exist in vain
Drop me off this eternal drop
I will join the Gods of despair
And never return back...

Good friends this is our journey's end
I thank you all for the time you have spent.

About The Author And Illustrator

Dr. D. Ronald Hadrian is a professor, author, and freelancer. He has published four novels and has contributed to various anthology publications. He is the founder of DRH Academy which provides skill based courses for schools and college. He reads and writes extensively. He is very active on LinkedIn and hopes to write more books, poems, and stories.

LinkedIn: Ronald Hadrian

Immaculate Nancy M. is an illustrator and works as an Assistant Professor. She fell in love with literature and writing at an early age and has been making continuous efforts to polish her skills, especially in writing and sketching. She has proofread numerous theses and documents and has also undertaken translation work

Insta ID : nancy_lawrnce